CW00622057

CUT TO THE CHASE VISUAL EDITION

LEE, BAZ & FRIENDS

Authentic

MILTON KEYNES • COLORADO SPRINGS • HYDERABAD

First published 2009 by Authentic Media
9 Holdom Avenue, Bletchley, Milton Keynes, MK1 1QR, UK
1820 Jet Stream Drive, Colorado Springs, CO 80921, USA
Medchal Road, Jeedimetla Village, Secunderabad 500 055, A.P., India
www.authenticmedia.co.uk

Authentic Media is a division of IBS-STL U.K., limited by guarantee, with its
Registered Office at Kingstown Broadway, Carlisle, Cumbria, CA3 0HA.
Registered in England & Wales No. 1216232. Registered charity 270162

British Library Cataloguing in Publication Data
A catalogue record for this book is available from the British Library

ISBN 978-1-86024-733-0

Every effort has been made to trace the copyright holders of images and quotes.
The publishers will be glad to rectify in future any errors or omissions brought to their
attention.

Cover and internal page design by Lloyd Kinsley | Lard Designs
Contributing Photographers: Lloyd Kinsley, Lee Jackson, Sophie Collin, Irum Shahid, Larrie
Knights, Alessandro Campos de Paiva, Diego Medrano, Sue Anna Joe, Herman Brinkman,
Erik P.Zado Araujo, Myles Davidson, David Siqueira, Jean Scheijen & Bora Inceören
Print Management by Adare
Printed in Great Britain by Bell & Bain Ltd, Glasgow

thanks

Thanks to everyone who helped us with design, photos, quotes or just general advice. Special thanks to **Linda, Clare, Rhea, Lauren, Lloyd** (larddesigns.com), **Chris, Anne, John, Roy, Malcolm, Authentic, Paul, Jon, Matt, Justin, Nick, Dave, Kevin, Steve Gerali, Carl Beech, Steve Legg, Eric Delve, Jeff Lucas, Dave Hopwood** and **blokes everywhere!**

kinesthetic

auditory

digital

visual

auditory

LOOKS BETTER

SOUNDS BETTER

FEELS BETTER

MAKES LOGICAL SENSE

People learn in four main ways. They are – visual 'looks better', auditory 'sounds better', kinesthetic 'feels better' and auditory digital 'it makes logical sense'. And I realised after all these years that I am a strong visual learner. The proof of this was pretty sad really – I have spent hours putting album artwork on my iPhone!

The penny has dropped. So, being a visual learner who writes wordy books, I was itching to do something different, to find a more visual way of communicating some of the key themes in *Cut to the Chase* (with loads of other stuff thrown in too). So, here it is – read it, leave it in your bag/toilet, come back to it, don't even read it from the beginning if you don't want, but chew on it (in your mind!), don't skip over the bits that challenge you – re-read them, discuss them, blog about them and maybe even pray a bit. Who knows, we might learn something together rather than just spend our life on facebook :) Enjoy!

cut to the chase

The phrase 'cut to the chase' developed from cinema
terminology, where it referred to the act of switching from
a less action-packed scene to a more exciting sequence . . .
within the past 15 years or so, 'cut to the chase' has come to be
used outside of the film industry with the figurative meaning of
'get to the point'.

[Source: Mark Israel, http://alt-usage-english.org/,
'phrase origins', 'cut to the chase']

Why spend a whole book padding out a single idea like a lot of books, when sometimes we just need a few words to put into practise?*

LET'S CUT TO THE CHASE – NOT GET ANOTHER WARM BATH.

*How many times have you heard long talks and only remembered one or two ideas mentioned? I have done that with week-long conferences (!) – but those few messages that I did learn and put into practice have changed my life. There is some comfort in hearing long sermons, but can we really put into practice 8–12 life-changing messages a month? Let those that stick, stick. But most of all act on them.

I got the CDs from a recent men's conference in the UK and none of the teaching was related to any of the inner struggles that men have. It was all inspirational stuff about 'go for it' and 'deal with your past' a bit and 'go for it' and 'God loves you', yet not actually dealing with the nitty-gritty of being totally honest in a completely male environment. It was just weird! WHY IS THAT?*

*Probably because a leader can only take people as far as they have been themselves.

So, here we go . . . No easy answers here, just loads of real life stories, but above all an honest, real approach that will pull very few punches. No weird theories, just real life lessons. If you are easily offended, put this down now and go read *Have a Nice Time with Vague Spiritual Quotes* available at your local bookshop. **Are you up for it?** If so read on . . .

Before we ask you to journey with us into the honest land of *Cut to the Chase* we thought we should be honest with you, our reader . . .

A few weeks ago, Lee and I celebrated our fourteenth wedding anniversary. My mom asked me how I felt about the 14 years. Well, I wouldn't choose to be anywhere else. There are lots of reasons why. Maybe because Lee can still surprise me, or because he takes the time to be romantic, or because he always encourages me and makes me feel good about myself in an insecure moment, or maybe just because he will sit and paint his kids' toenails with pink nail varnish. And just in case you think that Lee is some perfect husband, and that we float through life on a sweet-smelling boat of perfection and happiness, let's have a reality check. He's just an ordinary bloke who hates mornings, likes to be in control of the TV remote, has been known to show signs of grumpiness, gets mad with his kids and would struggle to cook something that didn't come out of a tin. (Am I being too honest now?) And sometimes he really makes me mad. The great thing is, life is not about being perfect. It's about doing the best you can with what you've been given.

CLARE
Lee's wife!

What would be the most scary thing that a man could do? 'mmmm – how about letting his wife write an unedited bit about them in their book?!' . . .

You will have noticed if you have read any of this book, a vulnerability that is refreshing and scary depending on your perspective. The first time I met Baz, he came into a meeting where I worked to speak to a team of Christian community development workers. His friend had been killed in a motorbike accident, and Baz shared how he was feeling, encouraged us to be real with God about things going on in our lives and left to cry in his office. As a 'let's keep it together' kind of girl this was a shock – instrumental in me seeking help to sort out some issues in my life . . . but just in case you think I've mistaken him for some kind of saint, he can be incredibly frustrating – letting his insecurities hold him back at times, not believing in himself the way he should, impatient when things aren't moving quick enough or when he's focused, highly embarrassing when he gives people prophetic words in restaurants (spot me running to the toilet?) and, horror of horrors, pretty useless at DIY!

LINDA
Baz's wife!

WHEN ONE OF THE BIGGEST ROLE MODELS IN THE WORLD, DAVID BECKHAM, JUST AFTER THE BIRTH OF HIS FIRST CHILD BROOKLYN SAYS, 'I WOULD LIKE BROOKLYN TO BE CHRISTENED BUT I DON'T KNOW WHAT RELIGION YET', YOU KNOW WE ARE IN TROUBLE!

Lowell Sheppard has written: 'I am amazed at how many young men I meet who are nice ... Very much in touch with their intuition and emotions but boring. They have no drive. When pressed, they talk about dreams but have little determination to turn fantasy into reality' (*Boys Becoming Men*, Authentic, 2002). We hope the book encourages you and/or really annoys you! What is the point of writing a book that nobody remembers?

WE DON'T DO BLAND.

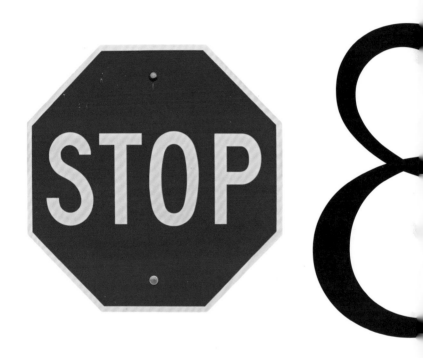

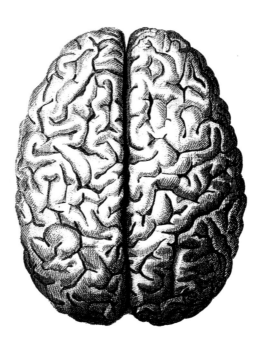

THE MOMENT YOU THINK OF YOURSELF AS GREAT

YOU HAVE LOST IT JIM COLLINS

WE ARE ALL ONE-PART PLONKER

... for thought.

It is no wonder that we have to write an honest book like this, because we have to deal with life differently now. Gone are the days when in order to see porn you had to go through the embarrassment of greeting (or stealing from) the local shopkeeper who knows your mum, or maybe worse, borrowing a dodgy mag off a friend!

Now most people, old and young, both in the workplace and at home, have **free** and **easy** access to Internet porn within a few seconds of switching on their computer.

In fact, while I am typing this at home right now, it would only take me a few seconds on a search engine and I could be immersed in a world of porn. The world has changed, so we have to as well. It is important to be realistic as well. Pornography isn't a fun thing which is passed around the office as videos were at my first job in a solicitors' office – it can be an extremely serious problem for a lot of men.

- **51%** of church pastors admit that looking at Internet pornography is their biggest temptation. (Christianity Today, December 2002)
- **37%** of pastors say it is a current struggle and four out of ten have visited a porn website. (Christianity Today, December 2002)
- It is also believed that **70%** of women involved in pornography are survivors of incest or child sexual abuse. (from www.xxxchurch.com)
- **40%** of couples in counselling say Internet porn is a problem. (Relate 2006)

Internet pornography is accessible, affordable and almost anonymous and it can appear secret and safe. Those who discover the joy in life from the sacred gift of sex will find the plastic substitute of porn losing its power over them.

Sex is brilliant!

But like anything else it can be tainted. A bit like a bad remix of a good song. It sounds so bad it puts you off the real song.

THOSE WHO LIVE ONLY TO SATISFY THEIR OWN SINFUL NATURE WILL HARVEST DECAY AND DEATH FROM THAT SINFUL NATURE. BUT THOSE WHO LIVE TO PLEASE THE SPIRIT WILL HARVEST EVERLASTING LIFE FROM THE SPIRIT.

GALATIANS 6:8, NLT

DID YOU KNOW
THAT WE CAN
NEVER **'FALL
FROM GRACE'**
(SEE ROMANS 8:1)
AND THE
GRACE OF GOD
COVERS ALL

Often we change jobs, friends and spouses instead of ourselves

Akbarali H. Jetha

Until you make peace with who you are, you'll never be content with what you have
Doris Mortnan

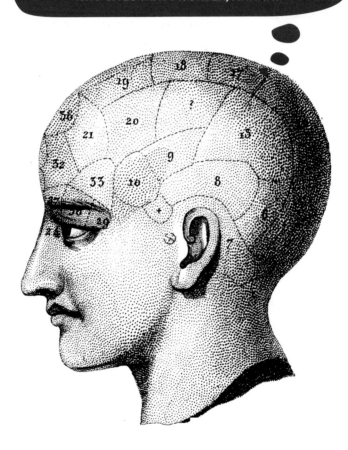

I HAVE NEVER KNOWN CONTENTMENT— I AM FOREVER IN PURSUIT AND DON'T KNOW WHAT I'M CHASING

HAROLD ABRAHAM FROM THE FILM *CHARIOTS OF FIRE*

TWENTIETH CENTURY FOX FILM CORP., 1981

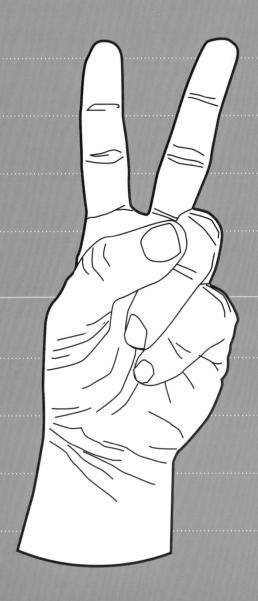

FRUSTRA-TION IS AN-OTHER WORD FOR ANGER

DAVE LOGSDALE

PAST

PRESENT

DON'T LET THE PAST
DICTATE YOUR FUTURE
BUT LET THE FUTURE
DICTATE YOUR PRESENT

MARTIN SCOTT

Every sunrise is a
second chance
Susie J

I wake up every morning
based on positive energy, that
the day's going to be better
than yesterday
Will Smith

The best way to learn
to be a good leader is ... ⟶

Please go to page **64**

To escape criticism – do nothing, say nothing, be nothing

Elbert Hubbard

The worst moment for an atheist is when he is really thankful and he has nobody to thank

Dante Gabriel Rossetti

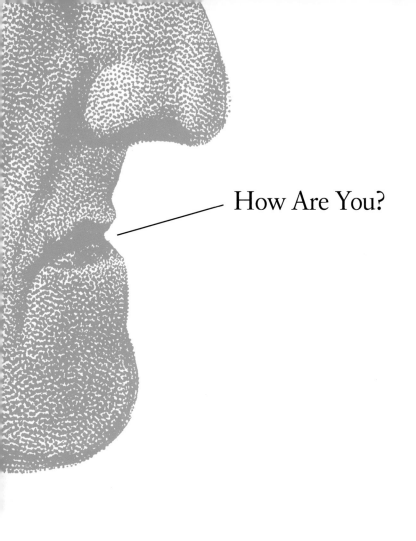

How Are You?

Feelings Inside Not Expressed OR

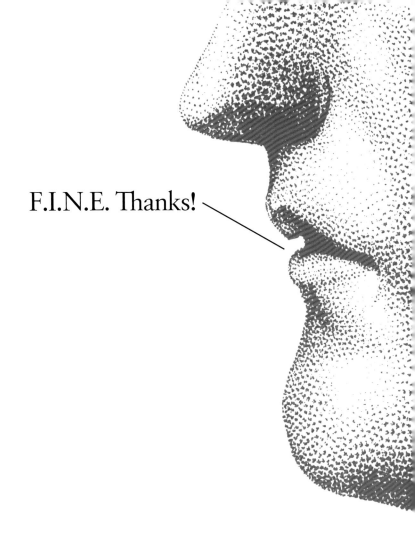

F.I.N.E. Thanks!

Fed-up* Insecure Nereoutic and Emotional

*this is the nice version of this phrase!

FINE

Well, as you probably guessed I am on a mission to ban the word **'FINE'** in the church today. Why? Because the good news of Jesus is not for **'FINE'** people. It's for people who are broken, helpless, who are in pain physically and emotionally. It's for the lonely, depressed, angry, bitter, the struggling, people with addictions and fears without hope or a purpose. It's for people carrying un-forgiveness in their lives and who are bogged down with their sin. It's for the bereaved, misunderstood, the wealthy and the poor. Whatever condition the person's life, heart and mind is in, this is who Jesus is for and not a bunch of people who are **'F.I.N.E.'** . . .

FIVE

I think of a bloke I met at a recent church gathering who always seemed very cheerful and 'FINE' when you asked him, but who recently committed suicide. Obviously, he wasn't as 'fine' as he appeared. We need to create an environment where people can come with all their crap and be accepted and loved to such an extent that it will encourage them to open up and begin to let God into the areas that need healing and forgiveness.

There is the well-known saying: 'People need to feel they belong before they believe and before they behave.' But for too long the church has said: 'You need to believe and behave before you belong.'

*(**Get Real**, Mal Fletcher, Word Books, 1993)

We need to create places where it's OK to be honest; where leaders are leading by example and showing that it's OK to be vulnerable.

I want to encourage you to take a risk and express what is really going on in your life with someone you know, trust and love and begin the process of unravelling all that baggage squashed inside that is bursting to get out.

'PEOPLE ARE NEVER MORE INSECURE THAN WHEN THEY BECOME OBSESSED WITH THEIR FEARS AT THE EXPENSE OF THEIR DREAMS.' — NORMAN COUSINS

A man who is fine will not achieve anything or feel fulfilled as a man; a man who is real, transparent and vulnerable will become a man. The man God intended him to be.

FINE

I try to travel on the train as much as I can to save petrol and it gives me time to think. You start in the flashy new station, everything looks good, coffee and bagels are flowing, it's busy and looks businesslike, but as you pull out of the station you see the other side. You see the tracks that have been closed down, the sidings that are overgrown, the redundant buffers, and the old carriages that are rusting away. There is graffiti everywhere on the outbuildings. Then as you go into the countryside, you see scrapyards and the backs of people's houses.

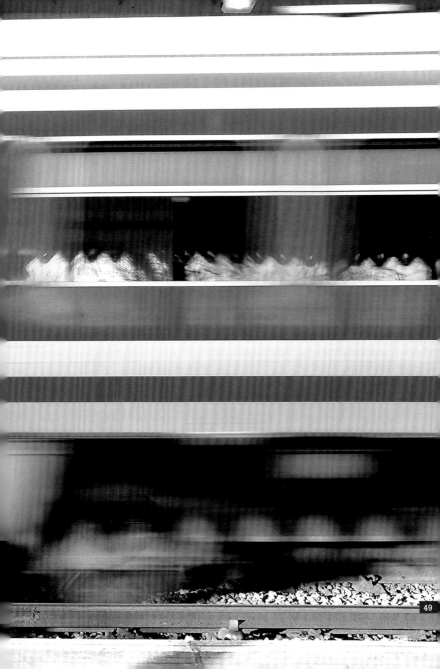

We often let everyone see the nice bits to our character but at some point we do need to let someone see the other parts of us as well – the parts of us that are not so nice, the thoughts we shouldn't be thinking, and the things we shouldn't be doing. If we don't deal with the darkness, we are simply not going to survive, like so many I have known. I have lived a semi-public life as a leader in Leeds for fourteen years now and I realise that there is a pressure when people know and recognise you around the place.

THE EASY WAY TO DEAL WITH THAT IS THROUGH GENUINE INTEGRITY, NOT TO PUT YOUR THINGS IN BOXES, BUT TO LIVE A LIFE WHICH SAYS, **'YES, I DO GET FRUSTRATED WITH MY KIDS IN THE SUPERMARKET BUT HEY, IT IS STILL ME!'** PERFECTION ISN'T THE GOAL, REALITY AND THEREFORE HOLINESS IS.

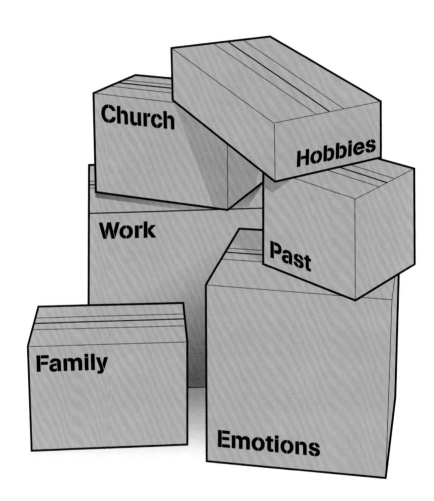

CAN YOU HANDLE THE PRESSURE OF INTEGRITY?

Duffy Robbins talked recently about a slippery slope in a mountain range in America. People think that they can ride downhill for part of it and then stop. But then they realise that they can't stop and people have gotten seriously hurt or killed on this slope. Once you take a few steps that's it, it's difficult to stop. If we are dabbling in stuff that we don't need to be involved in, we must not keep on doing it or it will get worse and we will go deeper and further. Give it to God now, talk about it with others and get it dealt with, plain and simple. It isn't rocket science!

Idi Amin, the infamous dictator of Uganda who died in 2003, was reported to be a complex character. He was responsible for up to 500,000 Ugandans dying directly from the orders that he had given, yet at the same time during his eight years in power, he seems to have had a reputation for being a practical joker. Bizarre.

In the Middle East, a Jewish settler broke into a mosque and opened fire with an assault rifle killing 29 Palestinian people. He was killed by the Palestinians around him after he had killed the people. His grave today is still a place of pilgrimage for many. On his gravestone it says, 'He was murdered for God, his hands are clean, he is a man of integrity.'

These are both extreme examples, I know, but as Duffy Robbins said, it only took a slippery slope to get there.

You can't blame the dark for being dark, you have to blame the light for not shining on it.

CRAIG GROSS, WWW.XXXCHURCH.COM

Shine Light Here.

Autopilot

I was in Leeds city centre, it was lunchtime so I grabbed a sandwich and a can of Coke while walking down Albion Street. I had a bag full of shopping, was balancing my drink precariously and enjoying the hussle of the city centre.

Then I saw a police van pull up in front of me and out of the back of the van jumped three policewomen, two of them went straight over to have a word with someone who was next to the bank on my left. This guy had a rucksack on his back and it was fair to say that he looked a little bit shifty. I was about 50 yards away when they asked to have a look in his rucksack. He took the bag off his back, then all of a sudden, started running. He pushed past the police and leapt over a pushchair, knocking the child over.

The child's mum, obviously shocked, started to go a bit mad. He stumbled towards me trying to get away and without thinking I punched him, pushed him to the ground and sat on him! I dropped my shopping and I kept my knees in his back as the police handcuffed him. They were obviously shaken by this incident as well and they put him in the back of the van. It was over in only a few seconds. The odd thing about it was that the police officers never acknowledged me or said anything to me, they just put him in the back of the van and then they drove off. I was frozen in the middle of town, my Coke had flown in the air, my shopping was all over the floor and I just stood there dazed, as the mum picked up the child in the pushchair (who was OK) and walked away.

I was stood in this daze in the street suddenly realising what I had just done. I genuinely didn't think about it, it was just something that happened and I was 'on autopilot' at the time . . .

As a contrast here is another Leeds man on Autopilot during the second world war . . .

One day, Smith Wigglesworth (Preacher and 'Revivalist') and James Salter visited Pastor Miles at his home in Leeds. Suddenly, Wigglesworth said to the two men, 'God is telling me to go to Ilkley Moor', he was speaking of a lovely town frequented by tourists about 16 miles away from Leeds city centre. Because of the war, petrol was rationed but Miles said he would have to drive them.

When they arrived they stopped at a lovely spot known as the Cow and Calf rocks, no soul was in sight so they seated themselves on an overlook. For some time, nothing happened causing Miles and Salter to think that Wigglesworth must have been mistaken, however, Wigglesworth had no misgivings and he was soon proven correct. A young man with a pack on his back appeared and sat down for rest next to Wigglesworth, soon the two were talking. The young man was a backslider who, like the prodigal, was disillusioned with sin. In a few moments there on the moor the man knelt with Wigglesworth and came back to God. 'What a prayer meeting we had that day on Ilkley Moor,' Miles later said. Then suddenly as before, Wigglesworth said, 'George you can take me back now I have done what God has told me to do.' (Albert Hibbert, *Smith Wigglesworth: The Secret of His Power*, Harrison House, 1993)

Imagine being tuned into God like Smith Wigglesworth, and God becomes your autopilot!

Smith
was a
plumber.

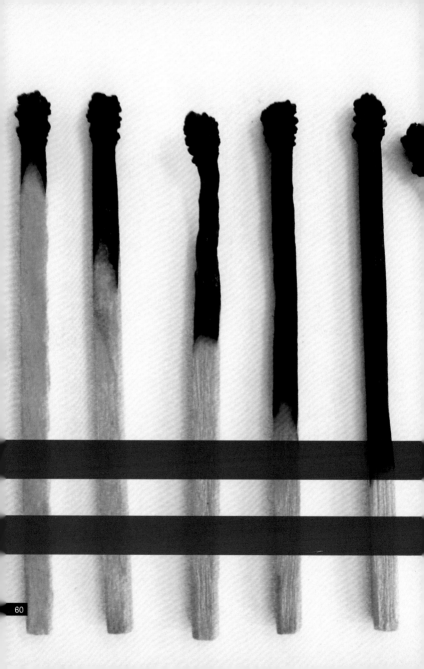

DON'T BURN OUT

KEEP YOURSELF FUELLED AND AFLAME

ROMANS 12:11, THE MESSAGE

ART
OR
SCI-
ENCE?

Growing up as a DJ, I have often discussed at gigs with other DJs and musicians whether DJing is an art or a science.

The answer is probably that it is a bit of both. There are certain technical skills that we have, but there is also an art in blending records, scratching and making sounds unique. Our faith is very similar, there is an art and science to it.

Some things are just fact and are unchanging, yet with some things, we need to be creative. We need to find a balance between the art and the science, the celebration and the suffering. They are part of the same package.

continued from page **39** ————————————▶

Please go to page **96**

PEOPLE PRETENDING TO BE PERFECT ARE NEVER HAPPY, THEY CAN'T BE, THEY ARE NOT PERFECT.

THERE IS FREEDOM IN KNOWING WE ARE NOT PERFECT.

Following God is sometimes just not wishing we were somewhere else. It's almost as if we have to 'suck the life out of that day' so we can see what God will do through us. The one thing we have the most control over is our attitude; as Charles Swindoll said:

Life is **10%** what happens to you and **90%** how you react to it.

Sometimes I think we over-spiritualise 'guidance' and create over-dependence on God. I think life is just about knowing who you are and getting on with it! I do wonder how the early church got on under the harsh conditions they experienced, where they put their lives on the line every day. Did they have a CD box set of seminars on guidance?

IF WE'RE AFTER SOMEONE WHO STANDS UP FOR THE OPPRESSED, WHAT ABOUT JESUS?

JEREMY CLARKSON

I WENT TO THE CHRISTIAN BOOKSHOP AND BOUGHT A RUBBER WITH A HIPPO ON IT – IT WAS MADE IN TAIWAN, PROBABLY BY A SIX-YEAR-OLD BOY MANACLED TO A RAIL.

AAARRRGH! If you're a dad, one of the things you need to understand is that all dads struggle.

Remember, most dads don't feel all the time that they are good dads, even if they are.

We are not on our own.

When doing a men's weekend a couple of years ago, one of the guys asked me if I would pray with him. He started to weep as he told me he felt he was short-tempered and negative towards his kids when they wound him up and he just wanted to be a calmer dad who smiled a bit more.

I could see that it took a lot of effort for him to speak to me about that. He opened up to someone about being a dad for the first time. We are all thinking at some point that we are probably not doing a very good job, but it is important that we are physically there – that's half the battle.

Although I have seen dads who are there but have an attitude that is so withdrawn they might as well not be there.

LIFE GOES BY PRETTY FAST.

IF YOU DON'T STOP AND LOOK AROUND ONCE IN A WHILE, YOU COULD MISS IT.

Ferris Bueller
Ferris Bueller's Day Off,
Paramount Pictures, 1986

GOLDEN BUTTS RD.

I have known my mate Andy for years and talked to him about God often but church was alien to him. He once told me that after I had invited him to a church social event we had on one night, he decided to come along, taking three buses all the way across Leeds, but when he got to the door of the church he looked inside and thought, 'These aren't my kind of people.' He turned around and went back on the three buses all the way home again. I never even realised he had got to the door of the church. I rang him the next day and he said, 'It's just not my thing, these people are different to me.'

We should look at our church through the eyes of a 25-year-old builder. That's when we get a new perspective on how strange we look to the outside world. Flowers, embroidered banners, singing lots of long love songs and very long non-visual talks with loads of jargon thrown in.

See Dave Murrow's book *Why Men Hate Going to Church* (Nelson Books, 2005) for more info on men and church.

andy

Andy made me think about how church looks to the outside world. A few years later our church started meeting for a while in a rough pub just a few hundred yards from his house, so I invited Andy one night as we worshipped and prayed 'in a pub style!'. Andy came along and he met God there one night.

When we were having a beer afterwards, he said to me, 'Something has just happened to me, Lee. I just feel like something inside of me has changed as I was singing that song.'

He didn't have the 'church jargon' to explain what had happened to him, that's what made it real to me. Andy made his first steps that night and he got talking to my mate Toby and others around church. He is still a part of our church community and now does some amazing volunteer youth work all over the UK.

GOD
Existence

There is one truth that helps to bring clarity
to academic debates about the existence of
God and it is this . . . 'God chose me.' Therefore
I didn't 'rationally' choose him . . . although I
could do, I didn't have to.

You are here
on purpose for
a purpose

'Even funeral cars die eventually,
so yes you may go grey and lose
your hair and there is nothing
you can do about it.

MOVE ON BALDY

WHEN WE **PRAY** WE **MOVE** OUR FEET

AFRICAN PROVERB

IF YOU, LIKE MANY BLOKES, GO TO SLEEP IN PRAYER MEETINGS THEN JUST STAND UP AND WALK AROUND. IT WORKS FOR ME AND KEEPS EVERYONE NERVOUS SO THEY STAY AWAKE TOO!

Baz prayer walked 350 miles once and he didn't close his eyes once! Laughing while praying is allowed. I was feeling very spiritual once at a conference and asked people to come forward if they were ill so that I and others could pray for them. After a few minutes a 20-year-old lad came forward looking a bit sheepish. I felt all spiritual as I asked him, 'What can I pray for?' His answer was straight to the point: 'I have got an ingrowing hair on me arse and it's got infected!' I prayed while laughing with him and explaining that I wouldn't be doing the laying on of hands, he agreed!

THE GREATEST OF FAULTS, I SHOULD SAY, IS TO BE CONSCIOUS OF NONE

THOMAS CARLYLE

We need to have a sense of reality in our prayers to God. As a man, it's important that you feel you can say whatever you want to God. When we are honest God meets us at our place of honesty.

During my journey with God, I have often shouted and sworn in anger, full of bitterness and even hatred to him, to do with feeling like a failure.

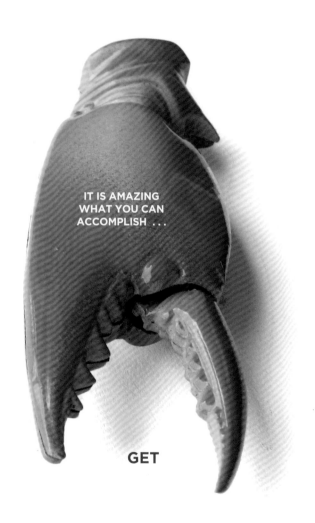

IT IS AMAZING
WHAT YOU CAN
ACCOMPLISH . . .

GET

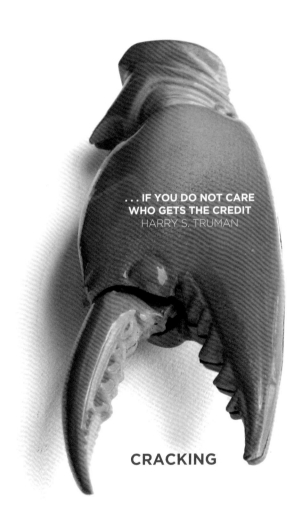

. . . IF YOU DO NOT CARE
WHO GETS THE CREDIT
HARRY S. TRUMAN

CRACKING

IF YOU WANT TO KNOW HOW TO LIVE YOUR LIFE, HELP YOUR FAMILY, RUN YOUR BUSINESS OR GROW YOUR CHURCH HAVE A LOOK AT JOHN 1:14

'THE WORD BECAME HUMAN AND LIVED AMONG US . . . FULL OF GRACE AND TRUTH.' (NIV)

IF WE CAN GET THIS
BALANCE I RECKON
WE'VE CRACKED IT.

91

LOVE AND TRUTH
FORM A GOOD
LEADER; SOUND
LEADERSHIP
IS FOUNDED
ON LOVING
INTEGRITY

PROVERBS 20:28, *THE MESSAGE*

FOOLS ARE HEADSTRONG AND DO WHAT THEY LIKE; WISE PEOPLE TAKE ADVICE.

PROVERBS 12:15, *THE MESSAGE*

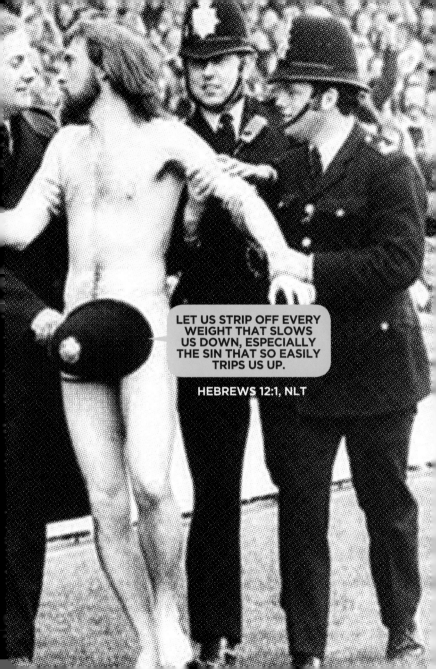

BEER IS
PROOF
THAT GOD
LOVES US
AND WANTS
US TO BE
HAPPY

BENJAMIN
FRANKLIN

continued from page **65** ───────────────➤

Please go to page **156**

God didn't create man for heaven. He created man for the earth.

MYLES MUNROE

God can't stand
deceivers, but oh how
he relishes integrity

more

✚

There is **nothing**
I can do to make
God love me **more**

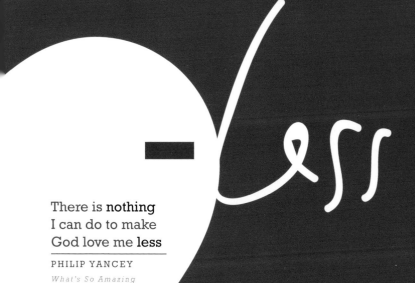

There is **nothing**
I can do to make
God love me **less**

PHILIP YANCEY

*What's So Amazing
About Grace?*
Zondervan, 1997

Does your church have **BMWs**?*

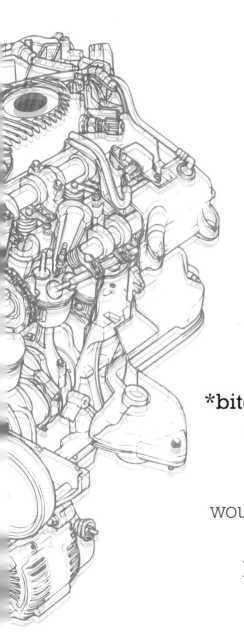

*bitches, moaners and whingers!

Many people would rather study the Bible than practice what it teaches

DUALISM? →

The number one thing that is attacked is the 'real you' and one of the biggest problems that we have today is the survival mechanism of what I have called dualism. It certainly is a major problem for some people in their teens and twenties in particular. When I was growing up, if I had done something wrong, then I was enormously guilty about it. I would feel guilty and sorry, apologising to God a thousand times and eventually coming back to God, half letting it go and then trying to get on with my life.

In order to survive this mad life, some people manage to 'put their lives in little boxes' (see p.51). There is a box which has all their church stuff in it, there is a box for work and there is a box for money and finances. There is also a box that has sex written on it. People have somehow tried to persuade themselves that this is how it should be. Everything should be in a little box and the boxes should never be opened and spilt into each other. If you fall out with someone you put them in one of the little boxes, seal it shut and rarely move on from it. This stifles the grace of God. For some people it is living one and a half, two or even more lives if it gets too complicated to manage. Also, the god of self comes into play. We persuade ourselves that 'I am the most important person in the universe. Everything should revolve around me and that's why I can have all these boxes, and my life is

→ WHAT IS IT?

not going to be challenged.' 'I like going to church with my friends, I like hanging out with people at festivals, but I don't really want it to spill over into the rest of my life thank you very much.'

I have seen dualism in action. I have seen people at major Christian festivals falling over in the Spirit, praising God, really getting into it, being swept along with thousands of other young people and then trying to have sex with a stranger the same night and, amazingly, they don't seem to see that maybe there is a conflict between the two. I would have been racked by guilt about stuff like that yet they can somehow justify or ignore it – true dualism, is like train tracks that never meet. Being dualistic can be a sign of a bigger issue – do we actually know who God is and what he thinks of us? It can also be a sign of poor discipleship and hurts from the past not dealt with. I remember I kept my music away from God for many years. I thought that he would never be interested in it and it was only when I completely handed my music and my DJing over to God that he really started to use me and I found out that he loved hip hop, which was nice.

Wrapped up in dualism, we can appear to be 'shiny' to certain people and look good to other people, but actually the way that we should live is in the open way that Jesus modelled. Remember that he lived in a community, where the houses were open or shared, there were extended families and probably no locks on the doors. There weren't very many places to hide away, unless you were a bored shepherd on a hillside. He lived his life in a very public and open way. We must strive for this kind of transparent lifestyle.

In Matthew 13, Jesus talks about the parable of the sower. The disciples were being really thick again and needed the whole thing explaining to them.

JESUS SAID TO THEM: 'YOUR EARS ARE OPEN BUT YOU DON'T HEAR A THING. YOUR EYES ARE AWAKE BUT YOU DON'T SEE A THING. THE PEOPLE ARE BLOCKHEADS! THEY STICK THEIR FINGERS IN THEIR EARS SO THEY WON'T HAVE TO LISTEN; THEY SCREW THEIR EYES SHUT SO THEY WON'T HAVE TO LOOK, SO THEY WON'T HAVE TO DEAL WITH ME FACE-TO-FACE AND LET ME HEAL THEM.' (MATTHEW 13:14,15, *THE MESSAGE*)

As I write this, I've just heard of a man I know who has had an affair and left his wife and young family. Our integrity is under attack, no doubt. Our first book, *Dead Men Walking* (now *Cut to the Chase 0.5*), was a call for genuine integrity not some weird patriarchal version of integrity that we have manufactured. Honesty and reality being the keys to genuine integrity and the ability to live your life in one big box.

THE ABILITY TO SAY TO PEOPLE 'READ MY MAIL', 'CHECK MY EMAIL', 'SURF WHAT I SURF', 'PARK WHERE I PARK', 'DO WHAT I DO' IS GENUINE FREEDOM.

As long as we don't allow it to disappear into legalism, it is genuine, genuine freedom. But we are not going to get there unless we have got one or two friends that we can be honest with.

IT'S THAT SIMPLE.

THE RITUAL OF WORSHIP WITHOUT SOME SERIOUS ATTEMPT AT WORTHY LIVING IS A PAINTED LIE AT BEST.
GEORGE BUTTERICK

So how do we survive this often crazy life?

One of the first things to remember is that our faith is a journey. This whole sense of journeying with God has really been lost in modern Christianity. If you have ever seen the film *Saved* (United Artists Films Inc., 2004) featuring Mandy Moore you will understand. In it, a right wing Christian college have a hard set of rules which everyone has to follow. They have forgotten that instead they should be journeying with God, not be in love with the rules that they think he gives, or even worse add their own twist to them. At one point, one of the young people starts to question her faith so they try to kidnap her and exorcise her of her 'demons' – she was just questioning a few things, but that did not fit into their religious regime.

WE ARE SIMPLY WALKING WITH GOD. SOMETIMES WE WALK CLOSELY WITH HIM, SOMETIMES WE HAVE GOT OUR BACK TURNED TO HIM (AND THAT MAKES IT REALLY DIFFICULT TO WALK!). SOMETIMES HE SEEMS DISTANT, BUT WE ARE STILL WALKING WITH HIM.

I think the Celtic saints showed us how to journey and walk with God very clearly. As we journey, the key to survival is understanding that we are under attack: the world, the devil, people around us are out to attack us in various ways. Always looking for the lowest common denominator, looking for common ground. Telling us we should buy everything we want because we deserve it, telling us that we should see as much porn as we can because we deserve it. We are men and it doesn't affect our lives. We should spend our money how we want to, deal with our businesses in the way that we want to. All this stuff is thrown at us every day and we need to be ready.

PROCRAS
TINATI

WE WILL TRY AND GET
AROUND TO THAT A
BIT LATER

I ONCE SPOKE AT A CHURCH IN SHEFFIELD

where a small brown envelope with the words 'For the preacher' written on it had been placed in the pulpit. I discreetly placed it in my pocket and carried on with the service. At the end of the service I left to go home. As I walked home, the sky turned grey and the heavens opened – thunder and lightning, the works. I got drenched but decided it couldn't get any worse so carried on home.

How wrong I was. After about three minutes walking, I stood in a massive load of dog crap covering not only the sole but also the laces of my shoe. How blessed I felt. This must be as bad as it gets. Oh no, the end of my trousers caught the big dollop on my shoe which rubbed itself in nicely. I eventually arrived home, wet, smelly and cold and desperate to get out of these clothes. After showering and warming up, I decided to open the envelope that was given to me by the church. How much had they decided to bless me with for the preparation, the service I had taken, plus costs incurred? I opened the envelope and a £1 coin fell out on the floor.

Friends of mine who did a concert were given a cheque at the end of the evening which didn't cover the amount agreed at the time of the booking. When questioned, the organiser replied, 'Oh don't worry, we have got you something else, seeing as it's nearly Christmas.' He then produced a box full of 200 mince pies. That's really going to help pay the bills! I asked my mate what they did with them. His answer made me laugh and still does today: 'We threw every bloody one out at the cars on our journey home.' Merry Christmas everybody!

Another friend of mine did a whole weekend for a church and they paid him with a small amount of money, some toilet rolls and a big lump of cheese!

EBENEZER SCROOGE IS ALIVE
AND WELL IN SOME CHURCHES,
PLEASE LET HIM DIE IN YOURS.

BLOOD

When I look at the blood all I see is love, love, love.

When I stop at the cross I can see the love of God

But I can't see competition

I can't see hierarchy

I can't see pride or prejudice or the abuse of authority

I can't see lust for power

I can't see manipulation

I can't see rage or anger or selfish ambition.

But I can't see unforgiveness

I can't see hate or envy

I can't see stupid fighting or bitterness, or jealousy.

I can't see empire building

I can't see self importance

I can't see back stabbing or vanity or arrogance.

I see surrender, sacrifice, salvation, humility,

righteousness, faithfulness, grace, forgiveness.

Love, Love, Love . . .

When I Stop! . . . at the cross I can see the love of God.

GODFREY BIRTILL

Some things in life are

These are the bits
we need to work on

INSA NITY

DOING THE SAME THING OVER AND OVER AGAIN AND EXPECTING DIFFERENT RESULTS.

ALBERT EINSTEIN

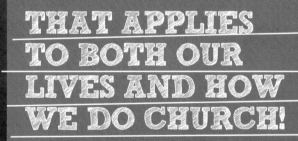

THAT APPLIES TO BOTH OUR LIVES AND HOW WE DO CHURCH!

shocked?

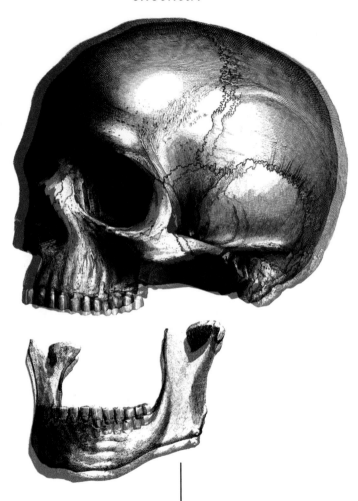

We're genuinely not trying to shock
We are just trying to be honest

*As our friend Jeff Lucas said to
a bunch of leaders recently*

MORE REALITY = LESS BURNOUT

THOMAS
EDISON: 'FATHER OF THE
MODERN WORLD' (1847–1931). 'NO
ONE DID MORE TO SHAPE THE PHYSICAL
AND CULTURAL MAKE UP OF PRESENT DAY
CIVILISATION . . . HE WAS THE MOST INFLUENTIAL
FIGURE OF THE MILLENIUM.'* ONE OF THOMAS
EDISON'S 1,093 INVENTIONS WAS THE LIGHT
BULB FILAMENT, BUT IT TOOK HIM OVER
3,000 ATTEMPTS TO INVENT IT!
THAT MEANS 2,999 ATTEMPTS
AT GETTING IT TO WORK,
FAILED. HE WORKED
18-HOUR DAYS AND
ONLY HAD FIVE HOURS'
SLEEP A NIGHT.

SUCCESS/
FAILURE

* THE HEROES OF THE AGE: ELECTRICITY AND MAN.

IN MY OPINION
MICHAEL JORDAN MAY BE THE
GREATEST SPORTS STAR OF ALL TIME. HE
WON SIX NBA WORLD TITLES – THE MOST VALUABLE
PLAYER IN ALL OF THEM. HE WON THE NBA SLAM DUNK
CONTEST TWICE, CHANGING IT FOR EVER. HE SCORED 32,292
POINTS IN HIS CAREER. HE WAS, UNLIKE MANY PLAYERS
THESE DAYS, 'THE COMPLETE PACKAGE': HE HAD THE
GREATEST OFFENCE, STIFLING DEFENCE AND HE WAS A MEDIA
PHENOMENON, DOING FEATURE FILMS THROUGH TO CEREAL
ADVERTS. YET HE SAID THIS: 'I HAVE MISSED MORE THAN
9,000 SHOTS IN MY CAREER. I HAVE LOST ALMOST 300 GAMES.
TWENTY-SIX TIMES I HAVE BEEN TRUSTED TO TAKE
THE GAME-WINNING SHOT AND HAVE MISSED; I
HAVE FAILED OVER AND OVER AND OVER AGAIN
IN MY LIFE AND THAT IS WHY I
SUCCEED.'

Somehow, in this instant world of Pot Noodles, McDonald's and quick boiling kettles, where the National Lottery promises us the ultimate get rich quick scheme and we respond to spam emails believing that someone has left us £2 million if we could only send them £100 for an administration fee(!), the concept that failure strengthens us has been lost. Often, it is in failure that we learn to succeed. Some people even say that there is no such thing as failure, only feedback. These lads knew how to accept feedback.

> Paul says, 'I don't understand why I act the way I do. I don't do what I know is right. I do the things I hate.'
> ROMANS 7:15, CEV

But he also says, 'My friends, I don't feel that I have already arrived. But I forget what is behind, and I struggle for what is ahead. I run toward the goal, so that I can win the prize of being called to heaven. This is the prize that God offers because of what Christ Jesus has done . . . But we must keep going in the direction that we are now headed.'

PHILIPPIANS 3:13,14,16, CEV

What you love to do/are passionate about

What you were 'wired up' to do

What people will pay you to do

*bingo

Don't chase money.
Just be good at
what you do and the
money will follow.

Chris Moyles

Better to be ordinary and
work for a living than act
important and starve in the
process.

Proverbs 12:9, *The Message*

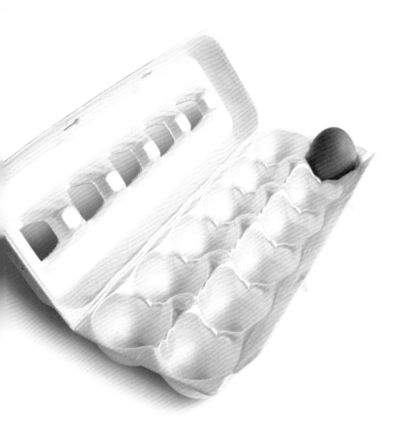

'THE OPEN DISCUSSION OF
LONELINESS IS THE MOST TABOO
SUBJECT IN THE WORLD. FORGET
SEX, POLITICS OR RELIGION OR
EVEN FAILURE, LONELINESS IS
WHAT CLEARS OUT A ROOM.'

(Douglas Coupland, from the book *Miss Wyoming*,
Random House, 1999)

I travelled to Norway to DJ at a gig a few years ago and I met
the guy who was the organiser of the event. He spent a bit of
time showing me around Norway in the winter – an amazing
place. As we talked, I realised that this guy was trying to follow
God but he was pretty lonely in his church. The church was
religious and he found going there very difficult. As he heard
more about my book, he really started to cry out for some
reality; he was desperate in his country, and his town, to find
other guys he could hang out with. There is still a need out
there, a need for reality and honesty – let's hope we can get to
people before they disappear.

HE'S TURNED HIS LIFE AROUND. HE USED TO BE DEPRESSED AND MISERABLE. NOW HE'S MISERABLE AND DEPRESSED.

David Frost

Our Man Cave may be our shed . . .

Most of us are not quite eccentric enough to actually have our own 'man shed' in the back garden. Maybe we might use our shed occasionally, like in the heartbreaking scene from the movie *The Full Monty* (Fox Searchlight Pictures, 1997) when Mark Addy's character, Dave, who is concerned about his weight, goes into the shed and wraps cling film around his stomach while eating a Mars bar, hoping that the weight will disappear.

We all need space, no doubt, and sometimes we really hope for a bit of peace and quiet, especially those of us that have young families. It doesn't mean we don't love them or we don't like them. It just means that we all need space, time to think and for some of us, time to pray as well. But it is easy for us to get lost in our sheds. For some people, it could be easy to spend their whole life hiding in there. I know that life is difficult sometimes, and we do need to get away from it all, but a lot of the time we need to tread this fine line between hobbies and mental illness very carefully.

Maybe sometimes when we do get stuck in our 'sheds', we need to give permission for other blokes to join us or even for other blokes to kick us out of the shed!

WE ALL NEED A GOOD KICK SOMETIMES!

GET OFF
THE VERGE

I was listening to a radio phone-in where an author was giving advice. One of the callers wanted to know how to go about writing a book he was thinking about. Immediately, the author interrupted and said, 'Easy. Stop thinking about it, get off the verge and do it.' He just kept saying 'get off the verge, get off the verge'.

Then the host Nicky Campbell got really animated as he suggested that this should be the motto for every person in the country thinking about doing something. 'Get off the verge, just get off the verge.'

I think the caller had got the message, as had I. 'Get off the verge and do something.'

WE DID

During my last year at Junior school we were asked to write about our summer holiday.

After lunch, back in the classroom, our teacher informed us he had had a chance to look at our work. He then went on to draw everyone's attention to a piece of work he had written out on the board, as an example of how not to write a story. I don't remember his exact words but something along the lines of the spelling being atrocious, punctuation poor and the whole thing being useless. All along I knew that he was making fun of my work, but when others laughed at the mistakes so did I, as I did not want people to know that it was mine. But it wasn't long before the class had to stop trying to guess whose work it was as our teacher decided to help them. He asked for the person whose work this was to stand up. So, as everyone was looking around, I stood, and as others smiled I began to smile to try and hide the hurt I was feeling inside. My memory of what followed had an effect on my life for over 30 years.

SON, I DON'T KNOW WHY YOU ARE SMILING. THIS WORK IS PATHETIC. WHY DO YOU BOTHER TO COME TO SCHOOL? YOU ARE AS THICK AS TWO SHORT PLANKS AND WILL NEVER ACHIEVE ANYTHING IN YOUR LIFE.

The class was laughing and I began to laugh and sway like a weeble, but inside I was feeling angry and wishing I could punch or head-butt him in the nuts. But I was only 10 years old. I do need to say that he was a good teacher. I enjoyed being in his class most of the year and had liked him until this point.

I still have many good memories of him and the class. I'm not sure if he'd just had a bad day or maybe his wife was not allowing him to have sex, but whatever it was I got the brunt of it that day.

AS THE OLD PROVERB SAYS,

THE TONGUE HAS POWER TO GIVE LIFE OR DESTROY IT.

In August 2006 we read in most of the national newspapers that the Revised Oxford Dictionary has 350 words to hurt and just 40 expressions to praise and encourage. 'Human nature being what it is, perhaps it's not surprising there are more words to convey negative feelings than positive ones,' said one expert at publisher Oxford University Press. It's easy to be negative – let's be people who speak words of life to people not death.

SOME MEN DON'T
NEED TO BE OUT IN THE
RAIN TO BE ALL WET

The most important person to be honest with is yourself

Draw a Self Portrait Here.

Christian leadership often consists of re-structuring, re-configuring, re-naming and re-branding. Anything that looks like something is happening but doesn't rock the boat, nor enable it to leave the shore.

Christian leadership often consists of **re-structuring, re-configuring, re-naming** and **re-branding**. Anything that looks like something is happening but doesn't rock the boat, nor enable it to leave the shore.

Acceptance.

Agreement.

These are not the
same – but they do
hold a key to many
relationships. We can
completely accept and
love someone without
agreeing with them
and their lifestyle.

WHAT DID I LEARN FROM CALVIN SMITH?

1

~~Ben Johnson~~

~~Carl Lewis~~

~~Linford Christie~~

(Calvin Smith)

2

~~Carl Lewis~~

~~Linford Christie~~

~~Calvin Smtih~~

At the **1988 Summer Olympics** in Seoul, **Calvin Smith** was involved in the most controversial Olympic 100 metres final of all time and ended-up receiving the Bronze Medal. **Ben Johnson** of Canada crossed the line first, with **Carl Lewis** second, **Linford Christie** of Great Britain third, and **Smith** fourth. But **Johnson** then tested positive for anabolic steroids and was stripped of his Gold Medal. **Smith** was thus upgraded to the Bronze Medal position. The race has been called the dirtiest race in history, as **Lewis** later admitted to having tested positive three times in that year's trials, and **Christie's** urine also contained metabolites of a banned substance after the race. Of the top 5 in that race, **Smith** is the only one who never failed a drugs test.

Well, most people, including myself initially, had no idea who had come fourth and then moved up to third place in probably the most famous 100 metres Olympic final ever. 'Baz, he may not have come first in the world arena, but he did finish and he did well and this is what I am wanting for you. It's not about having your picture in some glossy magazine, but it is about being faithful right to the end.'

3

~~Linford Christie~~

~~Calvin Smith~~

4

~~Calvin Smith~~

Shall I abandon, O King of mysteries,
the soft comforts of home?
Shall I turn my back on my native land,
and turn my face towards the sea?
Shall I put myself wholly at your mercy, without
silver, without a horse,
without fame, without honour?
Shall I throw myself wholly upon you, without
sword and shield, without food and drink,
without a bed to lie on?
Shall I say farewell to my beautiful land,
placing myself under your yoke?
Shall I pour out my heart to you, confessing
my manifold sins and begging forgiveness,
tears streaming down my cheeks?
Shall I leave the prints of my knees on the
sandy beach, a record of my final
prayer in my native land?
Shall I then suffer every kind of
wound that the sea can inflict?
Shall I take my tiny boat across
the wide sparkling ocean?
O King of the Glorious Heaven, shall I go of
my own choice upon the sea?
O Christ, will you help me on the wild waves?

ASCRIBED TO SAINT BRENDAN THE NAVIGATOR (BORN AD 484)
BEFORE SAILING ACROSS THE ATLANTIC IN A SMALL CORACLE.

ONE OF THE MOST IMPORTANT THINGS WE CAN DO IS TO BECOME 'LIFELONG LEARNERS', WE NEED TO FIND WAYS OF FEEDING OUR MINDS WITH STUFF THAT IS HELPFUL AND STRETCHING. IF YOU ARE A READER THEN READ, IF NOT FIND OUT HOW YOU LEARN BEST.

TIP:
SKILLS

SHAFT:
CHARACTER

FLIGHTS:
HOLY SPIRIT

AND DON'T FORGET
TO WORK ON YOUR
CHARACTER AS
WELL AS YOUR
GIFTS.
THERE IS NO POINT
BEING A GREAT
PUBLIC SPEAKER IF
YOU'RE NOT
A NICE PERSON TO
HANG OUT WITH.
SOMEONE ONCE
SAID IF YOU ARE
IN A RESTAURANT
WITH SOMEONE AND
THEY ARE NICE TO
YOU BUT NOT THE
WAITER,
THEY ARE NOT A
NICE PERSON.

WINE MAKES THE HEART OF MAN GLAD
PSALM 104:15

PROBLEM

'I like your Christ, I do not like your Christians. Your Christians are so unlike your Christ.'
MAHATMA GANDHI

SOLUTION

WYSIWYG

'Let your "Yes" be yes,
and your "No", no, or
you will be condemned.'

JAMES 5:12B, NIV

continued from page **97** ——————————▶

... to be a **Good Follower**

Followers make a
huge difference

JILL GARRETTT

ASK PEOPLE ABOUT GOD NOWADAYS AND THEY USUALLY REPLY, 'I'M NOT RELIGIOUS, BUT DEEP DOWN I'M A VERY SPIRITUAL PERSON.' WHAT THIS PHRASE REALLY MEANS IS, 'I'M AFRAID OF DYING BUT I CAN'T BE ARSED GOING TO CHURCH.'

COLIN RAMONE

I PROMISE YOU THAT YOU CANNOT GET INTO GOD'S KINGDOM, UNLESS YOU ACCEPT IT THE WAY A CHILD DOES.

MARK 10: 15, CEV

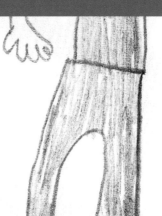

Rnea
Age 9

WE DON'T HAVE TO CHECK OUR BRAINS IN AT THE DOOR BUT SOMETIMES WE MAY NEED TO STOP DEBATING OUR THEOLOGY AND JUST HANG OUT WITH GOD A BIT, LIKE MY KIDS HANG OUT WITH ME.

Lauren
Age 9

My mother was not over keen on my new-found faith in God.

I can understand that having seen me six months earlier in hospital having my stomach pumped after taking a cocktail of pills and alcohol, she probably thought I was going mad. So, to try and keep the peace in the house, I used to hide my Bible notes inside the middle of a book entitled *The Man in the Iron Mask*. I had cut the middle pages out with a Stanley knife and slotted the

notes inside. I am sure she knew, just like I knew she hid the biscuits in the washer from my brother and me. My Bible was an old King James version which I had been presented with when I was at junior school.

Initially, reading the Bible was exciting as I wanted to discover more about Father God and Jesus and the way I was to live my life . . . But over the years I have seen myself reading the Bible for lots of different reasons, not

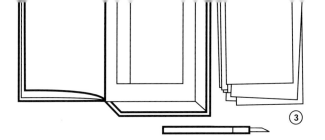

always good. At times, I have read it not for my own benefit but because I have been worried about what others would think if I hadn't read it for a few days, weeks or months. So I would read begrudgingly to appease my conscience. At other times, I thought that if I did not read it God would stop loving me.

And how many of us have fallen into the trap of 'unless I read my Bible today I will have a bad day'? Where does that sound familiar? 'Scorpio, you need to make sure you have a clean pair of knickers just in case!'

And what about Bible bingo where you just open it and hope that God will speak? That is until you do just that then read 'go and be circumcised' and with a grimace close your Bible and your legs.

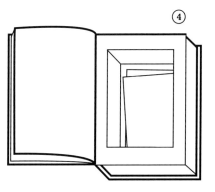

...the other danger

is that we read the Bible so that we can look more knowledgeable to others because of our vast understanding and the ability to quote the book and verse, maybe even holding our open Bible low enough so that others can be impressed with all our <u>underlining</u> and highlighting.

It's possible to worship and love the Bible more than we do Jesus. Then the Bible moves from being the life-giving word that points to our God, to becoming our god/superstition. I remember once when I felt so intimidated by how well-read other people's Bibles looked compared to mine that I spent 15 minutes throwing mine around, stamping on it trying to make it looked well used!

I love the Bible, as it's the Word of God, but we need to ensure we read it for the right reasons and not as a superstitious back-up to our day.

Things You **Need**

 Love

Rick Astley would **never:**

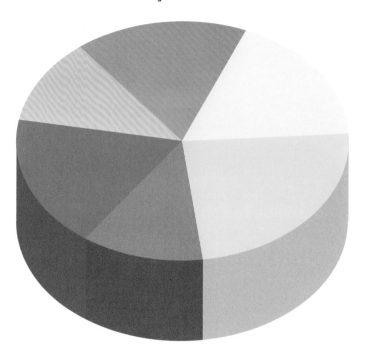

Give You Up

Make You Cry

Let You Down

Say Goodbye

Run Around and Desert You

Tell a Lie and Hurt You

I'm too shy to express my sexual needs except over the phone to people I don't know

GARRY SHANDLING

THE 'M'* WORD!

Someone once said to me, 'Lee, most Christian leaders hope
you won't ask them two questions:

1) How's your personal prayer life?

and

2) Do you masturbate?'

YOU WON'T HEAR THAT IN AN
ELDERS' MEETING VERY OFTEN!

Don't knock masturbation – it's sex with someone I love.

Woody Allen's character Alvy Singer
from the film *Annie Hall*, United Artists, 1977

A friend of mine once estimated how many times he had masturbated – and this had been a serious habit for him. The number was around 150,000 – no, it was, really! If the Victorians were right about their theories of the medical effects of masturbation, he must have contracted every disease known to mankind. He hasn't and they were wrong. It's embarrassing talking about it but 96 per cent of men have done it, and the other 4 per cent are probably lying. If we pretend it doesn't happen then we risk it becoming an unmentionable subject. But as me and Baz have started speaking at men's events, it is often the only issue that people want us to talk about! And it is the issue that they are expecting us to talk about, almost as if this is the only issue for men. Which it isn't of course.

to mas-

turbate

or not

to mas-

turbate

Each of us must formulate a personal view informed by factual evidence about sexuality and Scripture. Regardless of your viewpoint, there is freedom: freedom from guilt and shame, freedom to choose to engage or not and freedom from condemnation. Masturbation like all other wisdom issues, will provide one of three options for you:

1 You might call it sinful, in all cases.

2 You might decide that it is an issue of personal liberty, within certain boundaries.

3 You might see it as requiring continual discernment – because at times it may be right and at times it may be wrong.*

'Everything is permissible for me' – but not everything is beneficial. 'Everything is permissible for me' – but I will not be mastered by anything.

1 Corinthians 6:12, NIV

* Steve Gerali, *The Struggle*, Th1nk Books, NavPress Publishing Group, 2003. Used with permission

EVEN AS I SIT HERE SUPPING MY PINT I CAN BE **HIGH** AND **MIGHTY** ONE SECOND, **DOWN** AND **DIRTY** THE NEXT. I CAN ACHE TO **HEAL THE WORLD** ONE MOMENT, **UNDRESS A WOMAN** THE NEXT.

DAVE HOPWOOD,
THE BLOKE'S BIBLE, AUTHENTIC, 2006

Responsibility - Accountability = Liability

PHIL WALL

ONE OF THE GREATEST LIES THAT MEN BELIEVE IS THAT THE GRASS IS ALWAYS GREENER SOMEWHERE ELSE

In other words, 'If only I could do that then life would be better', 'If I was somewhere else right now life would be better', 'If I could only get that promotion then my life would be much better', 'If my girlfriend would only be like . . . then life would be so much better', 'If my church was more like this, life would be so much better.' But the fact is in life we have to decide to make the most of the moment we are in.

BILLY CONNOLLY ONCE SAID, 'THERE IS NO SUCH THING AS BAD WEATHER, THERE IS ONLY INAPPROPRIATE CLOTHING' AND I AM DEFINITELY WITH BILLY ON THAT ONE. YES, WE GO ON HOLIDAY AND IT'S NOT PERFECT AND MAYBE WE HAVEN'T GOT AS MUCH MONEY AS WE WANT TO SPEND AND MAYBE IT'S TOO HOT, MAYBE IT'S TOO COLD, BUT WE HAVE THE ABILITY TO MAKE THE MOST OF WHAT WE'VE GOT. WE HAVE THIS DECISION TO MAKE ALMOST EVERY MINUTE OF THE DAY.

PEOPLE GO FROM DENIAL TO DESPAIR AND MISS THE BIT IN THE MIDDLE

AL GORE

WE DO MAKE AN
IMPACT ON THE WORLD
WE LIVE IN. THIS IS NOT
A CHOICE WE MAKE.

THE CHOICE IS WHETHER
WE MAKE A **POSITIVE** OR
NEGATIVE IMPACT.

WE HOPE YOU ENJOYED OUR BOOK.

I STAND BY ALL THE
MISSTATEMENTS
THAT I'VE MADE!
DAN QUAYLE

IN THE END THERE
HAS TO BE HOPE.
DOUGLAS COUPLAND

notes

WANT MORE WORDS?

CUT TO THE CHASE 0.5 is an updated and remixed version of the ground-breaking men's book *DEAD MEN WALKING*. Seven years on, Lee and Baz are back with a totally re-written version of the book that pioneered the way for honesty and reality in books for men. With ten new chapters, plus updates of their favourite ones, this is a true remix of an out-of-print men's classic that was written as a brutally honest and raw account of what it is to be a man today.

'This book is raw, rude, offensive, gripping, occasionally gut-wrenching, with an honesty that will leave you breathless and a call that could seriously mess up your life – in the best possible way.' – **from the Foreword by Jeff Lucas**

CUT TO THE CHASE Encouraging men to discover what it means to be truly masculine. Packed full of quotes, humour, information and true stories, it's raw, gritty and a breath of fresh air.

'There are few books available in the Christian press that combine this level of honesty and inspiration written in a very entertaining, down-to-earth way'
Revd Paul Maconochie, Senior Leader, St Thomas' Church, Sheffield

'A fast-paced, punchy, down-to-earth and funny read that does what's on the label – it gets right to the heart of what matters.'
Jeff Lucas, author, speaker, broadcaster

'This has to be one of the world's bravest books . . . Thank God, then, for the honesty and humour of this new book from my good friends Baz and Lee. Baz and Lee are the real deal – funny, friendly, passionate, faithful, honest, imperfect and kind.'
from the Foreword by Pete Greig

AVAILABLE FROM YOUR **LOCAL BOOKSHOP**,
FROM **WWW.LEEANDBAZ.COM** (WITH FREE AUDIO BOOK) OR
WWW.AUTHENTICMEDIA.CO.UK